Praise for Spoil

'In these poems Morag Smith gives utterance to Cornish fore-mothers, the silenced exploited 'Bal Maidens' of 19th century tin mining. Her driven vehement pared-back lyricism also speaks to the widespread poverty of present-day Cornwall that goes unnoticed by tourists. This is a poetry of witness. A forceful linguistic acuity brings to life her time spent living road-side as a New Traveller, with her young children. This is an original and brilliant debut.'
  - Penelope Shuttle, *Lyonesse*

'*Spoil* transcends what we know about Cornwall and leads us somewhere deeper. A visceral telling of Smith's own history, coupled with that of the working landscape's. It gives me goosebumps every time.'
  - Jennifer Edgecombe, *The Grief of the Sea*

'Morag Smith's dynamic *Spoil* shows the earthy underbelly of Cornwall, one preoccupied by land and capital, and who has access to it. Meet the 21st century, rabbit-skinning, 'queens of the road', driving their trucks to another site 'hemmed in by dark curves of gorse', with the 'landscape emptied', where 'The whole idea of home / disintegrates'. Meet the 18th century bal maidens, girls and women breaking stones above the mines, worked into the ground, 'like I ain't felt the fist'. In Morag Smith, Kernow has a powerful, essential, contemporary poetic voice.'
  - Katrina Naomi, *Wild Persistence*

SPOIL

Smith

ISBN: 978-1-913642-69-3

Cover design by Aaron Kent

Edited by Jennifer Edgecombe

Typeset by Aaron Kent

Broken Sleep Books (2021)

Broken Sleep Books Ltd
Rhydwen,
Talgarreg,
SA44 4HB
Wales

Contents

Sky Disk   9
Heligan   10
Elvis the Enforcer   11
Rabbits   13
Leaving   15
Eye on the Mirror   18
Salt of the Earth   20
Prima Materia   21
Great Flat Lode   22
Empty   23
Ictis   24
Morning Rain   25
The Bal Maiden Breathes Out   26
Eliza Allen Truro March 10th 1841   27
Copper Mine   28
Carn Brea   30
Fire in the Hole   31
Forks   32
Cold Night   33
Infinity Pool   34

Acknowledgements   35

Spoil

Morag Smith

Sky Disk

Sky disk. Guide me back to the Island of Tin. *Cassiterides. Ictis.*

Cornish tin in the bronze of seven stars, the metal magnetized, drawn back to the place it came up. 300 million years lying like a blanket over its bed of rock. Granite that cooled and formed, long before that mineral flow poured into the cavity left by decomposing stone.

The sky disk's a heavy, blue-green eye looking for the route; it wants to go back, rest in the dark. It has worked for so long, 5,500 years mapping the paths of stars, moon, and sun.

I want to go home to the Island of Tin. *Cassiterides, Ictis.* It pulls me, calls me, the minerals in my blood leading me South West.

I look at the stars through a circle of finger and thumb.

Heligan

This dark place
is mud-bound
Underground
Sub-stratum
of a sub-culture
Found in rough bark
memories of goats
       stiff white hair
       spiking my small hands
       its wild pale eye
       arranged around a small black window
       from which it watches
Found in damp smell
       leaves breaking down into mud
       houses membraned in mould
Found in the dark
       a canopy filtering light
       night walk
       obscurus
       feet finding the edge of the path
Found in the squeak
       of a wheelbarrow
       cutting through mud
       one wheel caking as it cuts

Elvis the Enforcer

The sour weight of unripe apples
bends the bough
We drive from farm to farm
awaiting a harvest
that never comes
diesel diminishing
Everywhere's the same
not-yet
not-yet
We drive and drive
the diesel
di-minished
fruit un-picked
pick pick
unravel
beg the shop to tick me
a packet of nappies
some bread
a few vegetables
pick pick
unravelled parts of me trail
like string
a line
on the road
Mevagissy
Heligan
an old woodyard
at the edge of the woods
its dry border
blowing away in a hot wind
Elvis the enforcement officer
his empty threats
handwritten
flutter
a flag flying from
the rolldown back of the van

Then he takes tea by the fire
with our babies
crawling in the dust
they hang on his knees
he likes the feel
of the fireside
but abides in belief in his job
He finds the land rights
ownership issues
our common is landfilled
left and uncommonly
owned by no-one
He leaves
we stay
The summer is unusually hot

Rabbits

Her trailer leans
old tins on the floor
windows sift dirt from the wind
obscuring the light
'me and you'
she says
'we're queens of the road'
wonders why
she had to teach my son to skin a rabbit

I walk on the dunes
with my German friend
her black hair lifts up
white skin
dotted with red
either side of her tiny nose

Earlier
at home
short legs kicking back
against a damp bale of hay
watching me cook
Betty tells me
as she lights the end of a stick
that she wants to eat a rabbit
She's four years old
gazing into the distance
imagining how it will taste

The wind blows sand
into a soft scoop of dune
filled with a roll of thorns
a pocket
carved by the breeze
a death cry
briefly drowning out the sound
of waves breaking
on a beach we can't see

My friend's proud dog
drags a rabbit from the brambles
lays it at my daughter's feet
takes just the eyes
The child watches as I
grasp its strong back legs
the tendons
like guitar strings
under its silky coat

We walk home
As it swings
the body cools
They watch me
chop its feet and peel its skin
translucent
blue white glow
inside a soft brown furry glove
the dog can have its head
Betty hefts the little axe
but misses
cuts its ear in two
a neat triangle
clean   flat
and strange

Leaving

I climb in first
and light a blaze of candles
throw a log in the burner
our shadows leap
onto the walls around us
there are kids all over the place
quiet
waiting

The oldest
nervous
runs the edge of his tracksuit
between his finger
and his thumb
I hear the gentle zip
his skin
against the nylon ribs
I count
to ground myself
…3 4 5 6

Sitting on the rug
his sister leans her head
against his leg
– thumb in
twisting a curl of hair –
he reaches down
lifts her
sits her on his lap
eyes closing she lies back
he holds her
but I know
right now
it's her that's holding him

His head hangs
eyes shine in shadows
looking up at me
He doesn't need to say it
the enemy he made
came today
like a snarling dog
meanly slinking round
the yard
stood in the mud
told us
we had a week
to leave
before he came to burn us out

Around his boots
our footprints filled with water
Today *no-one* called him Captain

We all just stood
hands hanging loose
staring
without questions
We'd thought that we could stay
make it home
had planted Gunnera by the stream
I turned away without a word
went inside my truck and shut the door

'We leave tomorrow
Get up with the sun
tat down
I've found someone else
to drive my van
Ben will hook
the trailer up to his
I'll take the truck
We won't be back
pack well
we go at twelve
and leave whatever's left'
– then we put the little ones to bed

I drive out in the dark
leaving children guarding children
so I'm certain of the route we'll take
Walk up the lane
slowly cut the lock
that holds the gate

Eye on the Mirror

Up here
above the road
I'm a fucking queen
I'm scared to death before we go
but the engine fires
and I'm taking my foot off the clutch
really slow 'cause
I've got ten tons of truck behind me
and kids everywhere

It hisses like an old-time-train
as the air
escapes the system
starts to creep slowly forwards

How do I know
how long
how high
how wide I am?
Wearing this truck
like an armoured avatar

I do though

I can take it down our little lanes
round cars
through gates
over lawns
past signs
past the anger of strangers
who throw themselves in the road
to stop me

But up here
once we're away
and I'm driving

I never want to stop
I want to drive to
the edge of the land
then on
to India
Afghanistan
Finland
My back straight
perched on the edge of my seat
feet just reaching the pedals
arms spread wide
gripping the width
of the steering wheel
eye on the mirror
waiting for the inevitable
blue light

Salt of the Earth

Don't call me salt
call me soil
call me dirt
call me unrefined

Behind me
the hill rises up
but under me
the ground is broken

Grubbed in the dark
holder of seeds
turn shit black
I am the fifty foot woman
up to my neck in it

when I merge
into the ground like this
I appear smaller
but be wary
of the depths I sink to

Aiming my eyes at the earth
I look into the dirt
see the disturbances
beneath the surface

The past pulses
through my boots
making the buckles rattle
The Bal maiden
her history
the sorting and sieving
freezes the blood
in my veins
winds up lodged
under my fingernails

Prima Materia

The mother that made me
         was mud and stone
I was cut from rough rock
            raw and ragged
crusted in quartz
Lay on her great
granite belly
a cliff
folded by birth
like an impossible mattress

Whole galaxies
       gleam in the afterbirth
spread out around the stone
darkening the earth
       Ore
spills from veins
          that split
     and spit
         metallic clots
into the space
that opens up
between
the rocks

Great Flat Lode

All around
uncapped shafts
create slight depressions
in the ground

Spoil
rising gently to the lip
once heaped up
now falls stone by stone
into the dark beneath
chased by echoes
down long walls
of rough rock

Once a man stood here
vanning the land under the hill
standing on rich soil
building a counting house in his mind

Now the surface is
slag
waste from ore
hauled to the light
broken up by men
then spalled
by freezing girls

Empty

On the slopes around the town
sparse gorse and heather
frame stained rock
The grass won't grow
and spoil shows through

People shuffle home
between discount clothing shops
and the seven eleven off-licence

Smoking their spliffs
on ruptured sofas
Forgetting to put the bins out

Long forceps deliver their children
onto the worn carpet

You can't culture rock and stone
the ground's been turned
burned and broken
the landscape emptied

They seek emergency housing
in the old factory
where frames hold up walls
hiding heaps of rubbish
broken bikes
fragments of an old TV

Ictis

Mark the angle between the blue-green patina
and an inlaid rainbow
melt the metal crescent and the stars
the sky disk is a milky moon
refine it   refine it
cast it into a solar barge

This is a stranger century
a promontory island
Ictis

Chalcolithic metal workers
converse with veins of earth
dig out a small portion
refine it   refine it

Uncertain civilizations
between Belerion and the Mediterranean

These are the moon people
forging ancient island tin
Bronze weapons brought to the sun

Cast a molten arc along the ground
golden symbols
the strategic importance of care

A cluster
of seven metal workers

Morning Rain

Bal Maiden I

'I ain't complaining'
she hugs herself in the thin light
before the sun is properly up
A chilly wind
wraps wet skirts
round short legs
pain in her flat chest
She's cold as the bucking iron
she holds in small strong hands
Staring out
from under her bonnet
at the rain
running
off the bucking plate
waiting for the Captains shout
to start the day

The Bal Maiden Breathes Out
Bal Maiden II

After they blast the rock from her face
and fill up the kibble
I smash it to dust with me short hammer
its egg-shaped head whistles through air
thick with smoke from furnaced coal and wood
wood from forests dense as woven cloth
but now stripped bare
a lady with her dress took off
and here's me
cobbing her bits like I don't know
breaking her up
smashing her face
like I ain't felt the fist
like I don't know she hurts

Eliza Allen - Truro, March 10th 1841

Bal Maiden III

Eliza Allen twenty years old
finds it hard to stand
feet wet
she can't work the hours she's given by the mine
disorder of the system leaves her short of breath
makes a second pair of boots
impossible to buy

Two years she's worked
cobbing her delicate constitution
can't read or write
spends the day sitting down
breaking rocks
Finds it difficult to keep her feet dry
and always catches cold when she does not
breathing problems mean
that she don't sing
with the other women
as they open up the stone

Copper Mine

Bal Maiden IV

The men rag the rocks
pass them on
broken up
Women spall with long hammers
smash it more
search for the bits
that hold the ore they want
pass it on
They're strong enough to break the stone
stand in a long line
voices harmonize
hymns rise over the never-ending
sound of rocks breaking

They complain of the cold
wet boots
their bodies aching as they work

Little girls picked
washing and sorting
drenched from head to foot
finding the different ores
in what was smashed to bits by their elders
A filthy job
without the need for strength
pass it on for the cobbing
Stronger girls
short hammers swinging
breaking it to the size of a fingertip
singing to god
and passing it on for bucking

Only the most robust
wield the flat faced bucking iron
crushing the cob to powder
on the bucking plate

making it ready for smelting
Barrowed away by a pair of girls
pushing one and a half
hundred weight between them
in a wooden barrow

Carn Brea

We look for the palm print
on a great boulder
balanced
at another time
ready for hurling
on a shoulder of granite
that shrugs itself free
from rough green cloth
a paisley
of last year's bracken

The giant paused here
long before men found copper
in the water she wore
skirting the hill
Light entered the clear stream
caused multiple suns
to shine from the flow

Later she watched
as the spoil
of her hard flesh
piled up
While under the surface
she was destroyed

Fire in the Hole

Deep tunnels
fill with dark water
Impassable catacombs
and culverts

where men once waited
in the half light
for the blast
to shake them

      *

Mines
are empty churches
The silent bell tower
no longer smokes

Forks

I want to go home
                    but keep unpacking
The whole idea of home
disintegrates when I touch it

I build houses from light
their frames shake with the weight
of huge waterwheels
hanging from their crumbling sides

fat sheets of dark water
fall into deep stone troughs
more real to me than the houses

The silver forks and painted bowls
are lost in a garden of green
disc shaped leaves
that grow all winter
in the shade at the back of my truck

A red petrol tank
from a dead motorbike
                             hangs in a tree
near the genny
                like a diseased fruit

My dream-self packs boxes
while another part of me
hunts for lost forks
under a rising green tide

Cold Night

Silver skin of condensation freezing my fingertips
as I slide the window open
lean out smoking
watch my neighbour's windows
looking for familiar silhouettes
their trailers white in the small light of distant stars
A circle of vehicles
hemmed in by dark curves of gorse
The old mine site empty of dog walkers

My sons and their friends
smoke bongs behind Rasta flag curtains
burners blazing
muffled laughter escapes thin aluminium walls

Next door a half-built house
the man who told the press we ruined his dream
lives in the garden with his wife and children
the house for sale
to finance relocation
somewhere warmer

BOOM

Like a massive firework
our torched car
lights up the vans
I stand with my sons
watch long flames burn for hours
emptying a fire engine

firefighters finally bury it
shovelling earth into its gutted frame
tutting about arson

Infinity Pool

The infinity pool has no edges
as it laps the horizon

Learn to touch
with the in and the out breath

A construction industry
involuntarily abandoned

fragments of capitalism
broken scaffolding

We swim inappropriately
in this borderless pool

our fingers reaching
for the sky

swimming harder
trying to touch that impossible line

Acknowledgements

First I must thank my children, for their love, patience, and encouragement. Rupert Loydell for starting me writing poetry again and for his enlightened, editorial eye. Luke Thompson, for taking me to Bodmin Moor Poetry Festival to hear and be inspired by live, contemporary poetry. Penelope Shuttle, a great friend, who recognised my real voice and helped me find the confidence to use it. Caroline Carver, for friendship, food, and inspiration. Katrina Naomi, for giving me permission to write against the rules and in forbidden territories. Gary Matthews, best proof reader ever. Jennifer Edgecombe, who helped me edit these poems and made the whole process alive and vital. Falmouth Poetry Group, who took me into their community of writers. My brother Sam, for lifelong love and support. Ian Franklin, for always listening. My mum, Brigid, and dad, Campbell, for immersing me in poetry from an early age. And finally Aaron Kent, for giving me the chance to share my work.

The Bal Maiden Poems originally appeared at Wild Court.
Eye on the Mirror originally appeared at the 2020 National Poetry Archive.

Apertya dha ankres